The Fading of The Day

Poetry by Cat Webling

Table of Contents

Dedicated to the people who keep me sane.
Special Thank You to Little Infinite Poetry.

I pray on my beads
Hail Mary, Hail Mary, Hail Mary, Hail Mary, Hail Mary,
Hail Mary, Hail Mary, Hail Mary, Hail Mary, Hail Mary,
Are you even there?
Do you hear me and pretend not to care?
Even that would be easier
Hail Mary, Hail Mary, Hail Mary, Hail Mary, Hail Mary,
Hail Mary, Hail Mary, Hail Mary, Hail Mary, Hail Mary,
The beads shake in my hand
As I struggle with all my might to understand
And hold on to slipping faith in fear
Hail Mary, Hail Mary, Hail Mary, Hail Mary, Hail Mary,
Hail Mary, Hail Mary, Hail Mary, Hail Mary, Hail Mary,
The world needs you
I need you, too
Is there anything out there?
Hail Mary, Hail Mary, Hail Mary, Hail Mary, Hail Mary,
Hail Mary, Hail Mary, Hail Mary, Hail Mary, Hail Mary,
Listen to me
Say something
Say anything
Hail Mary, Hail Mary, Hail Mary, Hail Mary, Hail Mary,
Hail Mary, Hail Mary, Hail Mary, Hail Mary, Hail Mary,
But there was no response

I walk among the ghosts
And in their silence, I see
Wasteland left behind

You kiss my lips
A whisper in the dark
In the quiet and starlight
As you pull me too close
But never close enough
And when dawn breaks
And the light filters in
You'll be gone like a dream
Where I wake up too soon

I float adrift at sea
In the waves
Thousands of boats
Like mine, small, in the dark
Crying out to each other
But too scared to touch
Bearing the stormy night
Weathering the pain
As some capsize
And sink into the waves
The survivors call from the ink
Beg for a hand
To be saved from the cold
But no one reaches for them
For fear of being pulled
Into the depths

I am so aware
Of the space between us two
But you're worth it all
□

Listen to you laugh
As you run for your friends
For a day
Watch you play
For a while
In the sun

When you throw back your head
And you yell to the sky
Turn your eyes toward me
And the smile on your face
Is a state of grace
Like a lottery I've won

And you run to me
Put arms around me
Call and ask for me

Turn to me without a reason
And tell me hello
Just to tell me you love me
Just to let me know

God you'll never know
How much I love you
How much you changed my life
And lit it up
You chose me
And I can never thank you enough
You can have all of my love

Glass walls
Everywhere I look
To hold us back

Open spaces
Unburdened by us
Trial by emptiness

Simple joys
Taken too soon
A strange kind of grief
You feel far too late

If I could only run
No boundaries, no restrictions

But we have lost that freedom
Everything we knew has changed

So much is gone
All I want is to be safe
For me, my family, my world
Eventually, we will be okay

But this is our world now

Startling sunshine
Bright in the afternoon
Bouncing from the small waves
That flutter over the water
Bouncing from the fluffy wings
Of geese that chatter and babble
Bouncing from the feathery leaves
Of pine trees souring into the blue
Bouncing from the neon green
Scales of little lizards sprinting along
Bouncing along in the yard
That sings in the late day

Silence in the air
Screaming, railing, silent day
Painfully quiet

Pretty little trills
Lovely jumps and dives of sound
Soaring melodies

Stuttering fingers
That slip on well-tuned plucked strings
Making joyful noise

No virtuoso
With years of training am I
Yet I am happy

It is natural
To love a care-free sweet sound
With all heart and soul

I don't feel bad for you Pandora
I feel bad for your neighbors
Who watch the sky open up
And the demons fly out toward them

I don't feel bad for you Pandora
I feel bad for your family
Who told you again and again
Not to play with the gods

I don't feel bad for you Pandora
I feel bad for your home
That was plunged into darkness
Without any choice at all

But I do feel bad for you Pandora
I feel bad for you
Who toyed innocently with the idea
That she was on top of the world
Who listened again and again
To folks saying "Sit down, be quiet"
who was plunged into darkness
Without any choice at all

Someday
When we are old
And we sit together
In sunlight chairs
We will look back
At today
And smile
Like this is nothing

Someday
When we are old
And I am by your side
As we fall asleep
We will look back
At today
And smile
Like this is nothing

Someday
When we are old
And I cheer you both
From the sidelines
I will look back
At today
And smile
As I have always done

I walk empty streets
I wander, alone
In the aftermath
Of whatever this is
I wander in the sun
And smell the Spring air
That might as well not be there

In my travels I find
A child on a bike
She rides by
On the far side of the street
And it's better this way
For both of us

I find a man with a dog
On a normal walk
And I cross the street
But smile back
At the pup on a leash
That wants to greet me
On another day, he would

I walk empty streets
I wander, but not alone
In the aftermath
Of trying very hard
To stop whatever this is
We wander in sun
And smile at Spring air
Glad that it is still there

This time last year, we gathered in the morning
To sing simple hymns and pass around colored eggs
We celebrated without thought to a warning
Of the question of certainty, the future often begs
We ran through the fields that lined family places
In bright colored dresses bough just for the occasion
We didn't worry we were too close, didn't count paces
And a little thing like a hug goodbye didn't take
persuasion
We didn't know back then what we know right now
And looking out the window at the waiting streets out
there
Would we change the way things are, would we want to
know how
This happened, back then, want to even be made aware
No, we wouldn't have wanted to know this strange new
cold
Because although they didn't glitter, those days were gold

Pity for the Devil 'cause he earned the world's scorn
For the envy of big brother when little brother's born
'Cause Daddy put a brand new picture up there on the
fridge
And Big Brother couln't stand the snotty little bitch
And I pity little Lucy who ran up to God to say,
"How could you love them when you made me this way?"
And God looked him in the eye and said, "Boy try again,"
And Lucy pissed him off so down the Devil's road he
went
Now the little snake have been and gone to Hell in a twist
But there's an opportunity he saw that wasn't to be missed
The snake penciled Eve in for the very first sin
And he took her to the damnedest place right 'longside of
him

In this lonely space
I can be with myself
And hold council
As I watch the world
Pass me by

I can stay in this place
And let my mind wander
To places forgotten
And bring them back to me

And when I am ready
I can open the doors
And return to the world
That moves so quickly

But for now, I am here
Alone with myself
And court is in session

Light a candle for your love
At the altar's side
And wait for them faithfully
All the long, dark night

Light a candle for your home
At the altar's side
And go back to it knowing
You'll be safe tonight

Light a candle for your country
At the altar's side
And go to do your duty
To protect it in the night

Light a candle for yourself
At the altar's side
And know that all you pray for
Is the safety of the night

It is warm
But not scalding yet
I can hear the birdsong
And the bees that buzz to work
The smell of the water
As it rises from the pond
For the first time in months
It's hot enough for that
Everything is in sharp detail
Sunlight striking
What was cleaned in the rain
So that it shines like gold
Red blooms on bushes
Whose names I've never known
Flowers drift in the air
Magnolia and wisteria
The light hits the ground
Like sparks from a flame
That will soon become summer
But not today, not in this moment

Simple heat
On summer streets
Like flames that strain
That ebb and gain
In comfort wish
Forgotten bliss
Yet once again we meet

Boxed in by words
Fenced in by defenses
I set my boundaries
In more ways than senses
I poured the concrete
On lines in my mind
So they're set in stone
And too easy to find
So maybe I'll be safe
From harsh words that I've heard
Echoing in my head
Mine and theirs blurred
If I box myself in
Build high walls and set stalls
To hide away in
When my doubt calls

Do not question the fading of the day
The ending of an era passing by
It is without reproach, without a sway

Gentlemen and their ladies often say
But far too often stop to question why
Do not question the fading of the day

A classic sits untouched in molded clay
No cause for battles long lost do they lie
It is without reproach, without a sway

And shelves and shelves of hist'ries line the way
To teach the world by unrepentant sigh
Do not question the fading of the day

And follow finely in that passion play
The gift of those far more well-versed than I
It is without reproach, without a sway

And you our course of study we must pray
Will guide through ages hence and ages nigh
Do not question the fading of the day
It is without reproach, without a sway

I wander paths worn by constant use
A wood with no clearly drawn trails
Unpaved, unsigned, no way markers here
Save branches a forgotten path hail
Scattered petals that show me
Older routes o'rgrown with time
Ways I have plundered to their depths
Clear'd mysteries but not wonders fine
Yet still my current trail I trek
To find new ways into this wood
Strike out from the way I have known
To see those things not now understood
Into the undergrowth and undisturbed sod
To places I have not yet eagerly trod

Lists, ideas, work, problems
Words that flow wrong on them
The pages write and write
Just to break the tide

Autocorrect is off
I can't filter my thoughts

From the shores I have seen
In summer-soaked childhood days
Lapping at the sand on islands
That stand alone against the tide
Changing and yet how it has always been
Changing island shores met in old ways
Changing the depths unproved and grand
The same unknowns our fears set aside
Centuries pass like minutes streamed
Unchanged by their changing plays
We ride and sail across our stands
Delving into the near depths untried
Poisoned by our actions but nonetheless
Our friend, adoring in the blue darkness

Catch a glimpse and hope to see
The swirls and speedy spirals
Fast-flowing lava, slow-moving stream
In feathery touches just beneath
When I laugh before I know what's funny
And cry before I know what hurts
In the spark behind my eyes of glee
Or the shine in my unconscious smile
More than muscle and electricity

My darling, here in my arms
Hallowed is your lovely smile
Thy glorious form has me undone
Here in our home which is our Heaven
Share with me your daily love
And bless me with trespasses
As you trespass with me
Lead me on into your temptation
Deliver me from the torture
Of missing your love

Call them weeds
These pretty little dandies
Say it all you like
But I like their way
Of sparkling in the sunlight
Call me a fool for spending
An afternoon in my yard
Picking out the pretty blooms
Little sunbursts on a string
Pretty pretty little things
So call them weeds all you like
Call them ridiculous
Show me your spite
But I'll be outside
Smiling at the faces
Of little rays of sunshine
Beauty in these simple places

What a wild open sky
Burning blue, shining high
This we welcome with a sigh

In they dance between the blinds
And wander through the room
O'er piles and pieces each foot finds
To rest among my books
Between the pages to recline
Or atop my many trinkets
To run a hand along each spine
And slowly fade them with use
Or perhaps to rest and sing
Upon my dusty guitar
And beg of me to pluck a string
And play a long forgotten tune
Or best of all, to come to me
As I lay asleep in bed
And tap my eyelids that I might see
Them welcome me to the day
What silly little spirits bright
Dance and flutter about my room
They are the dancing of the light
That make the flowers bloom

Honey, he will never fall
For the way you bat your lashes
You will wish you had it all
But it'll come to you in flashes
You will think that here and now
Is the be all, end all event
But honey, you cannot guess how
The next few years will be spent
You think right now your plan is set
In stone and bulletproof
You think it's as good as it'll get
You think you're so cool and aloof
Honey, when it hits the fan
And your world starts to crumble
You'll pick up pieces of broken plan
You'll try to walk but you'll stumble
I promise you honey, despite it all
You will make it out alive
And it will feel like a close call
But you will find a way to survive

you are
how i am
        striving

you are
where i am
        comfortable

you are
when i am
        happy

you are
what i am
        wanting

you are
who i am
        missing

Ten minutes ago I was naive
Nine years old and trusting that
Eight hours a day would be enough
Seven days a week would be enough
Six ways to say "I'm brilliant!"
Five fingers grasping a false future
Four points on a bullet list that got shot down
Three times I was knocked to the dirt
Two times I was lost in the pain of it
One way forward

I cannot go back so I'll grow
From all the things I can't let go

On some distant sunny future day
When the world has changed around me
When I am old and well-lived and grey
And my grandchildren will run to see
And I will tell them of the past
When the world made very little sense
When my days seemed to go far too fast
And my calendar days were far too dense
And they will ask me to tell them tales
And of course, I will indulge them
I will tell them how when one plan fails
Along comes a new and unexpected gem
I will smile and hope for these dears
The future is better and brighter and kind
There won't be a place in life for fears
And there will always be a joy to find
Yes, this is what I hope is the way
When I am old and well-lived and grey

I gave myself away, leapt out
Blindly, trusting I would be caught
By the ones I loved as I fell

I didn't listen
I should have

The first time gave me bruises
As I scrambled on the rocks
I saw hands grabbing for me and
Stumbling before I joined them
And was warned not to jump again
Because they might not be able
To catch me again

I didn't listen
I should have

The second time gave me scars
I saw hands folded at their sides
And I fell, and I broke
And I looked up and asked why
And was told in heartache tones
"I did everything I could"
As I bled on the ground below

I didn't listen
I should have

Here lie the ghosts
Of worlds we built
From uncut rubble
To shining cities

Long-gone posts
Standing on silt
Far gone trouble
They have my pity

Too many loose ends
Where laughter chokes
Echoing too-cold draft
An unattended mass

Phantom friends
And forgotten jokes
Of days we laughed
Through rose glass

My children are not playing
In the streets I keep for them
My children do not run around
The parks I've always leant
My children are not celebrating
Their liberty from the schools
My children have all disappeared
And I don't know what to do

My people are not walking
On the streets with busy sound
They do not go into their yards
And grills aren't crowded 'round
My people do not rush to swim
They don't jump in swimming pools
My people have all disappeared
And I don't know what to do

I try to tempt them out again
With long, warm, and sunny days
I try to give them cause to smile
But it does not seem to phase
I miss the sounds of laughter, too
On my streets in years gone by
My people have gone missing
And I don't know what to do

About the Author

Cat Webling is an author based in middle Georgia. She started writing professionally in 2018, when she published her first novel, Artificial Intelligence. She continues to write from her home, which she shares with her mom, dad, little brother, and lovely dog.

If you like her work, you can find her here:
@CatWebling on Twitter | @catwebling on Instagram | KittyCatThang on YouTube | Cat Webling on Facebook | The Bookshelf at **www.catwebling.com**